MW01173167

HOMESCHOOL PLANNER *and* ESSENTIAL ORGANIZER

- Undated Original -

Everything you need to plan, organize and track your homeschool year

Visit our website at **www.HomeschoolLifePress.com**

How to use this Planner

Every homeschool family has different needs and finding a planner that works well for your family is often difficult. That's why this planner has been designed with flexibility in mind. Some homeschoolers may start in August or September and follow the public school schedule, while others homeschoolers may start in January or any other month of their choosing. Some school for 9 months and take 3 months off, others school year round with many large breaks throughout the year. Many homeschoolers don't follow a traditional Monday - Friday schedule and instead school on days that work best for their family. For these reasons, this planner has been left blank and undated so it can be fully customized for each individual homeschool family's needs.

As a homeschool mom myself, I've never been satisfied with any planner system I've bought at the store. I've spent lots of money on teacher planners that don't always translate well for homeschoolers, and after a few years of frustration, I started making my own. I've also listened to the needs of my fellow homeschool moms, and created this homeschool planner to be flexible enough to accommodate most homeschoolers.

Whether you have one child or many, school year-round or follow a traditional public school schedule, have homeschooled from the beginning or have just decided mid-year to start homeschooling for the first time, this planner will help you track all the necessities and stay organized all year long.

Happy Planning!

Dawn

This planner/organizer is packed with extras that make planning easy, keep tracking quick and efficient, and keep you organized all through the school year. There are even budget sheets if you need to keep up with your school supplies and expenses.

- YEAR AHEAD
- TERM GOALS
- MONTHLY GOALS
- ACCOUNT TRACKER
- PASSWORD TRACKER
- FIELD TRIP TRACKER
- MONTHLY PLANNING
- CURRICULUM & RESOURCES
- MONTHLY DASHBOARD
- LESSON PLANNINER
- STUDENT CHECKLIST
- ATTENDANCE CHECKLIST
- BUDGET TRACKER
- READING LIST
- NOTES
- HOMESCHOOL CONNECTIONS
- YEAR IN REVIEW

To see samples of some of these pages in use, head over to my blog at **HomeschoolLifePress.com** to see page demos and planning tips

the essentials

The first section in this planner is ***The Essentials***. Here you will find easy reference pages to store important information you'll need all year:

- ***Curriculum and Resources:*** This can be a curriculum wish list, or a place to track your resources. If you are like me, and have more resources than you can keep up with, this can be a place to list everything you plan to use this year, paid or free. This section is divided by subject so you can see what areas may need more supplementation.
- ***Accounts:*** This was designed with online resources in mind. There are so many options out there and it's easy to forget useful resources you stumbled on and didn't write down. These pages can help you track your accounts, and keep up with renewals.
- ***Passwords:*** A place to store your logins and passwords for all your online homeschool resources.
- ***Reading List:*** Keep a list of all the books to read this year, mark off as you go.
- ***Field Trips:*** Keep your scheduled field trips here for reference or planning.
- ***Homeschool Connections:*** Keep the contact info of important homeschoolers and new friends you meet through the year.

the plan

The next section is called ***The Plan***. Here you can plan out your school year goals with ease.

- ***Year Ahead:*** These pages are kept blank so you can start with any month you want. It then breaks your year into quarters. You can use this to plan curriculum topics, or you can plan your breaks and vacation days. There are a number of ways you can use these pages and how you go about it is up to you.
- ***Term Goals:*** These pages break your year into 6 six-week terms for easy lesson and unit planning.

the schedule

The next section in this planner is ***The Schedule***. This is your yearly calendar.

- ***Monthly Dashboard:*** Each month begins with a dashboard that tracks your monthly goals, important notes, and to-do's. There's also a blank area that you can customize for your own needs, and a habit tracker that can be customized to track anything, from moods, to outside time, chores, physical education, field trips, or even grades or attendence.
- ***Monthly Schedule:*** Blank undated monthly calendar
- ***Weekly Lesson Plan:*** Blank undated weekly lesson planner that can track up to 5 days and 7 subjects. You can customize your day's of the week and subjects of study.

using the lesson planner

The lesson planner blocks are lined to help you neatly fit more info in less space. With 8 lines per block you could fit 2 lines of lesson planning per subject for up to 4 kids, 1 line for up to 8 kids, use all 8 lines for one child, or split them any way that works best for your family. Using color pens helps to keep everything organized if you assign a color for each child. We use the Frixion erasable gel pens to keep our planners color coded and neatly organized.

There are 5 blank weekdays for you to fill in your date and day of the week. For those who don't school monday - friday and instead use any other combination of days, this area was intentionally left blank so you could customize it around your unique schedule. There is plenty of room under the date for any important notes for that day.

Check out www.HomeschoolLifePress.com to find samples of the lesson planner in use.

tracking

The next section in this planner is ***Tracking***. This is where you will keep important records. Depending on which state you're from, some of these records are required by law. For the rest of us, it's great info to keep just in case you need it in the future.

- ***Attendance:*** Easy way to keep a tally on each child's attendance. For those who don't keep track of attendance this area can still be used as a habit tracker of your choice. There is enough space to track any habit you want everyday for a year.
- ***Student Checklist:*** Keep track of any important grades for your records, or use as a different checklist for those not tracking grades.
- ***Budget:*** Easily keep track of your homeschool costs.

review and reflect

The final section in this planner is ***Review and Reflect***. Here you can keep notes and thoughts about this school year. There are journal prompts to help you along.

- ***Year In Review:*** Your year's end journal with prompts to aid in writing.
- ***Notes:*** any extra thoughts you want to keep.

now let's get started....

When the atmosphere encourages learning, the learning is inevitable

- Elizabeth Foss

the essentials

- Curriculum & Resources
- Accounts Tracker
- Password Tracker
- Field Trip & Event Tracker
- Homeschool Connections
- Reading List

curriculum and resources

SUBJECT:

SUBJECT:

SUBJECT:

SUBJECT:

curriculum and resources

SUBJECT:

SUBJECT:

SUBJECT:

SUBJECT:

SUBJECT:

SUBJECT:

SUBJECT:

SUBJECT:

accounts

ACCOUNT NAME	PURCHASE DATE	EXPIRE/RENEWAL	PRICE

accounts

ACCOUNT NAME	PURCHASE DATE	EXPIRE/RENEWAL	PRICE

passwords

WEBSITE / ACCOUNT	LOGIN	PASSWORD	NOTE

passwords

WEBSITE / ACCOUNT	LOGIN	PASSWORD	NOTE

field trips

FIELD TRIP / EVENT	DATE	TIME	FEE

field trips

FIELD TRIP / EVENT	DATE	TIME	FEE

field trips

FIELD TRIP / EVENT	DATE	TIME	FEE

field trips

FIELD TRIP / EVENT	DATE	TIME	FEE

homeschool connections

NAME	PHONE	EMAIL

homeschool connections

NAME	PHONE	EMAIL

reading list

reading list

reading list

reading list

Education is not the filling of a pail, but the lighting of a fire

\- William Butler Yeats

the plan

- Year Ahead
- Term Goals

year ahead

1			
2			
3			
4			
5			
6			
7			
8			
9			
10			
11			
12			
13			
14			
15			
16			
17			
18			
19			
20			
21			
22			
23			
24			
25			
26			
27			
28			
29			
30			
31			

year ahead

1			
2			
3			
4			
5			
6			
7			
8			
9			
10			
11			
12			
13			
14			
15			
16			
17			
18			
19			
20			
21			
22			
23			
24			
25			
26			
27			
28			
29			
30			
31			

year ahead

1			
2			
3			
4			
5			
6			
7			
8			
9			
10			
11			
12			
13			
14			
15			
16			
17			
18			
19			
20			
21			
22			
23			
24			
25			
26			
27			
28			
29			
30			
31			

year ahead

1			
2			
3			
4			
5			
6			
7			
8			
9			
10			
11			
12			
13			
14			
15			
16			
17			
18			
19			
20			
21			
22			
23			
24			
25			
26			
27			
28			
29			
30			
31			

term goals

TERM 1	TERM 2	TERM 3

term goals

TERM 4	TERM 5	TERM 6

The home is the chief school of human virtues

- William Ellery Channing

the schedule

- Monthly Dashboard
- Monthly Calendar
- Weekly Lesson Plan

month

goals

to-do's

- [ ]
- [ ]
- [ ]
- [ ]
- [ ]

important

notes

DAILY TRACKER																			
1																			
2																			
3																			
4																			
5																			
6																			
7																			
8																			
9																			
10																			
11																			
12																			
13																			
14																			
15																			
16																			
17																			
18																			
19																			
20																			
21																			
22																			
23																			
24																			
25																			
26																			
27																			
28																			
29																			
30																			
31																			

MONDAY	TUESDAY	WEDNESDAY	THURSDAY

FRIDAY	SATURDAY	SUNDAY

NOTES

LESSON PLANNER

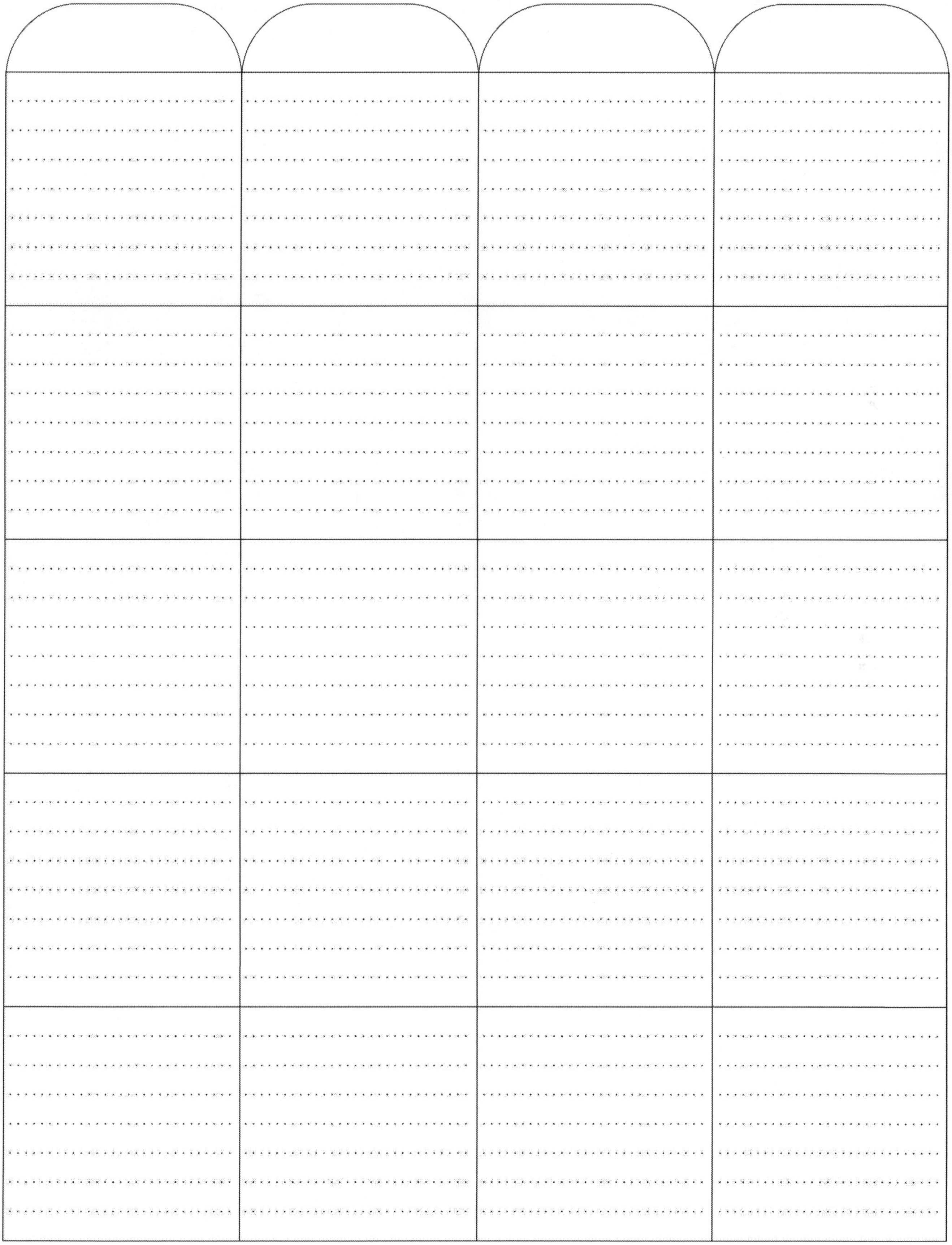

LESSON PLANNER

LESSON PLANNER

LESSON PLANNER

LESSON PLANNER

month

goals

to-do's

- [ ]
- [ ]
- [ ]
- [ ]
- [ ]

important

notes

DAILY TRACKER																			
1																			
2																			
3																			
4																			
5																			
6																			
7																			
8																			
9																			
10																			
11																			
12																			
13																			
14																			
15																			
16																			
17																			
18																			
19																			
20																			
21																			
22																			
23																			
24																			
25																			
26																			
27																			
28																			
29																			
30																			
31																			

MONDAY	TUESDAY	WEDNESDAY	THURSDAY

FRIDAY	SATURDAY	SUNDAY

NOTES

LESSON PLANNER

LESSON PLANNER

LESSON PLANNER

LESSON PLANNER

LESSON PLANNER

month

goals

to-do's

- [ ]
- [ ]
- [ ]
- [ ]
- [ ]

important

notes

DAILY TRACKER																			
1																			
2																			
3																			
4																			
5																			
6																			
7																			
8																			
9																			
10																			
11																			
12																			
13																			
14																			
15																			
16																			
17																			
18																			
19																			
20																			
21																			
22																			
23																			
24																			
25																			
26																			
27																			
28																			
29																			
30																			
31																			

MONDAY	TUESDAY	WEDNESDAY	THURSDAY

FRIDAY	SATURDAY	SUNDAY	NOTES

LESSON PLANNER

LESSON PLANNER

LESSON PLANNER

LESSON PLANNER

LESSON PLANNER

month

goals

to-do's

- [ ]
- [ ]
- [ ]
- [ ]
- [ ]

important

notes

DAILY TRACKER																			
1																			
2																			
3																			
4																			
5																			
6																			
7																			
8																			
9																			
10																			
11																			
12																			
13																			
14																			
15																			
16																			
17																			
18																			
19																			
20																			
21																			
22																			
23																			
24																			
25																			
26																			
27																			
28																			
29																			
30																			
31																			

MONDAY	TUESDAY	WEDNESDAY	THURSDAY

FRIDAY	SATURDAY	SUNDAY	NOTES

LESSON PLANNER

LESSON PLANNER

LESSON PLANNER

LESSON PLANNER

LESSON PLANNER

month

goals

to-do's

important

notes

DAILY TRACKER																			
1																			
2																			
3																			
4																			
5																			
6																			
7																			
8																			
9																			
10																			
11																			
12																			
13																			
14																			
15																			
16																			
17																			
18																			
19																			
20																			
21																			
22																			
23																			
24																			
25																			
26																			
27																			
28																			
29																			
30																			
31																			

MONDAY	TUESDAY	WEDNESDAY	THURSDAY

FRIDAY	SATURDAY	SUNDAY	NOTES

LESSON PLANNER

LESSON PLANNER

LESSON PLANNER

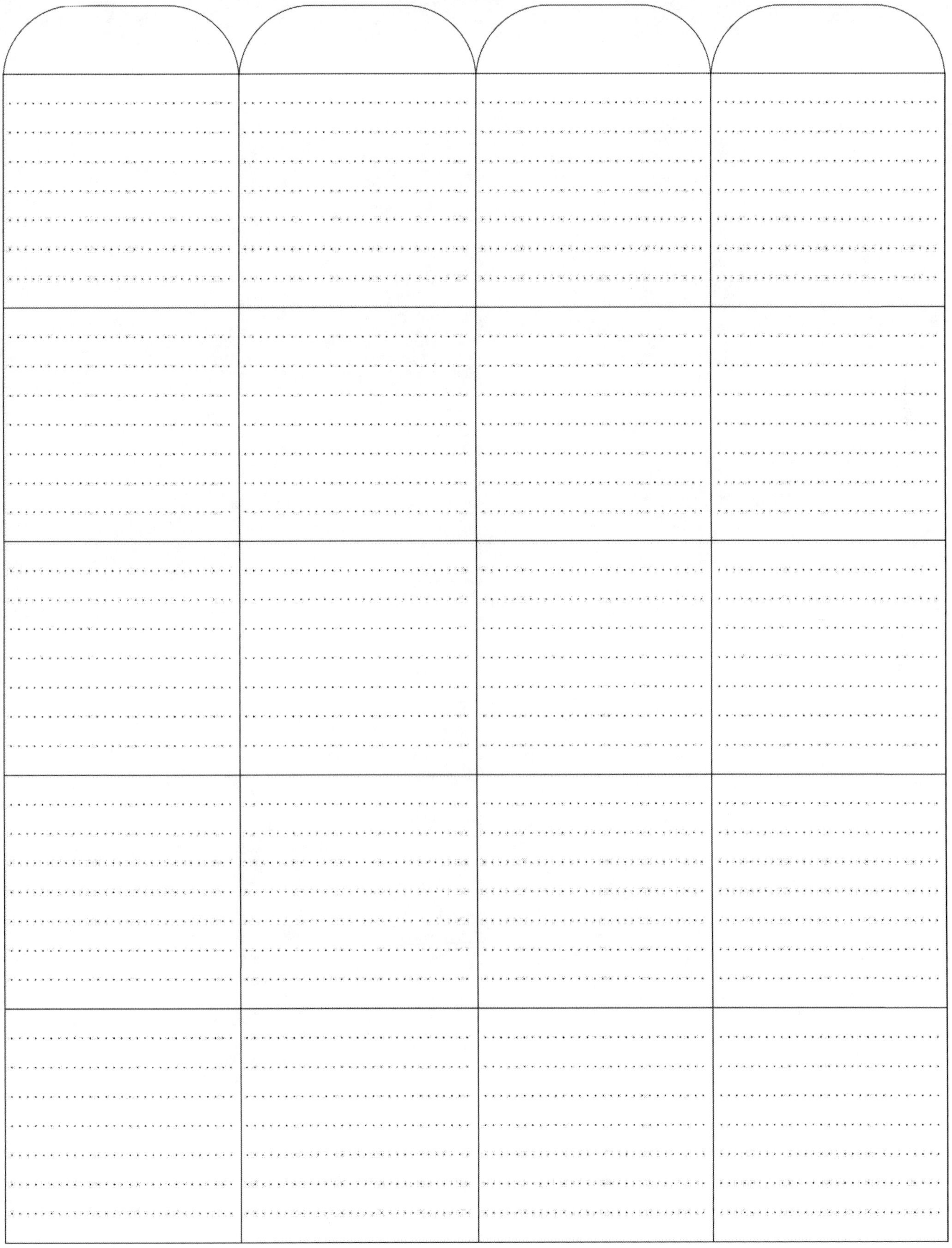

LESSON PLANNER

LESSON PLANNER

month

goals

to-do's

- [ ]
- [ ]
- [ ]
- [ ]
- [ ]

important

notes

DAILY TRACKER																			
1																			
2																			
3																			
4																			
5																			
6																			
7																			
8																			
9																			
10																			
11																			
12																			
13																			
14																			
15																			
16																			
17																			
18																			
19																			
20																			
21																			
22																			
23																			
24																			
25																			
26																			
27																			
28																			
29																			
30																			
31																			

MONDAY	TUESDAY	WEDNESDAY	THURSDAY

FRIDAY	SATURDAY	SUNDAY

NOTES

LESSON PLANNER

LESSON PLANNER

LESSON PLANNER

LESSON PLANNER

LESSON PLANNER

month

goals

to-do's

important

notes

DAILY TRACKER																			
1																			
2																			
3																			
4																			
5																			
6																			
7																			
8																			
9																			
10																			
11																			
12																			
13																			
14																			
15																			
16																			
17																			
18																			
19																			
20																			
21																			
22																			
23																			
24																			
25																			
26																			
27																			
28																			
29																			
30																			
31																			

MONDAY	TUESDAY	WEDNESDAY	THURSDAY

FRIDAY	SATURDAY	SUNDAY	NOTES

LESSON PLANNER

LESSON PLANNER

LESSON PLANNER

LESSON PLANNER

LESSON PLANNER

month

goals

to-do's

- [ ]
- [ ]
- [ ]
- [ ]
- [ ]

important

notes

DAILY TRACKER																			
1																			
2																			
3																			
4																			
5																			
6																			
7																			
8																			
9																			
10																			
11																			
12																			
13																			
14																			
15																			
16																			
17																			
18																			
19																			
20																			
21																			
22																			
23																			
24																			
25																			
26																			
27																			
28																			
29																			
30																			
31																			

MONDAY	TUESDAY	WEDNESDAY	THURSDAY

FRIDAY	SATURDAY	SUNDAY	NOTES

LESSON PLANNER

LESSON PLANNER

LESSON PLANNER

LESSON PLANNER

LESSON PLANNER

month

goals

to-do's

- [ ]
- [ ]
- [ ]
- [ ]
- [ ]

important

notes

DAILY TRACKER																			
1																			
2																			
3																			
4																			
5																			
6																			
7																			
8																			
9																			
10																			
11																			
12																			
13																			
14																			
15																			
16																			
17																			
18																			
19																			
20																			
21																			
22																			
23																			
24																			
25																			
26																			
27																			
28																			
29																			
30																			
31																			

MONDAY	TUESDAY	WEDNESDAY	THURSDAY

FRIDAY	SATURDAY	SUNDAY

NOTES

LESSON PLANNER

LESSON PLANNER

LESSON PLANNER

LESSON PLANNER

LESSON PLANNER

month

goals

to-do's

- [ ]
- [ ]
- [ ]
- [ ]
- [ ]

important

notes

DAILY TRACKER																			
1																			
2																			
3																			
4																			
5																			
6																			
7																			
8																			
9																			
10																			
11																			
12																			
13																			
14																			
15																			
16																			
17																			
18																			
19																			
20																			
21																			
22																			
23																			
24																			
25																			
26																			
27																			
28																			
29																			
30																			
31																			

MONDAY	TUESDAY	WEDNESDAY	THURSDAY

FRIDAY	SATURDAY	SUNDAY	NOTES

LESSON PLANNER

LESSON PLANNER

LESSON PLANNER

LESSON PLANNER

LESSON PLANNER

month

goals

to-do's

- [ ]
- [ ]
- [ ]
- [ ]
- [ ]

important

notes

DAILY TRACKER																			
1																			
2																			
3																			
4																			
5																			
6																			
7																			
8																			
9																			
10																			
11																			
12																			
13																			
14																			
15																			
16																			
17																			
18																			
19																			
20																			
21																			
22																			
23																			
24																			
25																			
26																			
27																			
28																			
29																			
30																			
31																			

MONDAY	TUESDAY	WEDNESDAY	THURSDAY

FRIDAY	SATURDAY	SUNDAY	NOTES

LESSON PLANNER

LESSON PLANNER

LESSON PLANNER

LESSON PLANNER

LESSON PLANNER

month

goals

to-do's

- [ ]
- [ ]
- [ ]
- [ ]
- [ ]

important

notes

DAILY TRACKER																			
1																			
2																			
3																			
4																			
5																			
6																			
7																			
8																			
9																			
10																			
11																			
12																			
13																			
14																			
15																			
16																			
17																			
18																			
19																			
20																			
21																			
22																			
23																			
24																			
25																			
26																			
27																			
28																			
29																			
30																			
31																			

MONDAY	TUESDAY	WEDNESDAY	THURSDAY

FRIDAY	SATURDAY	SUNDAY	NOTES

LESSON PLANNER

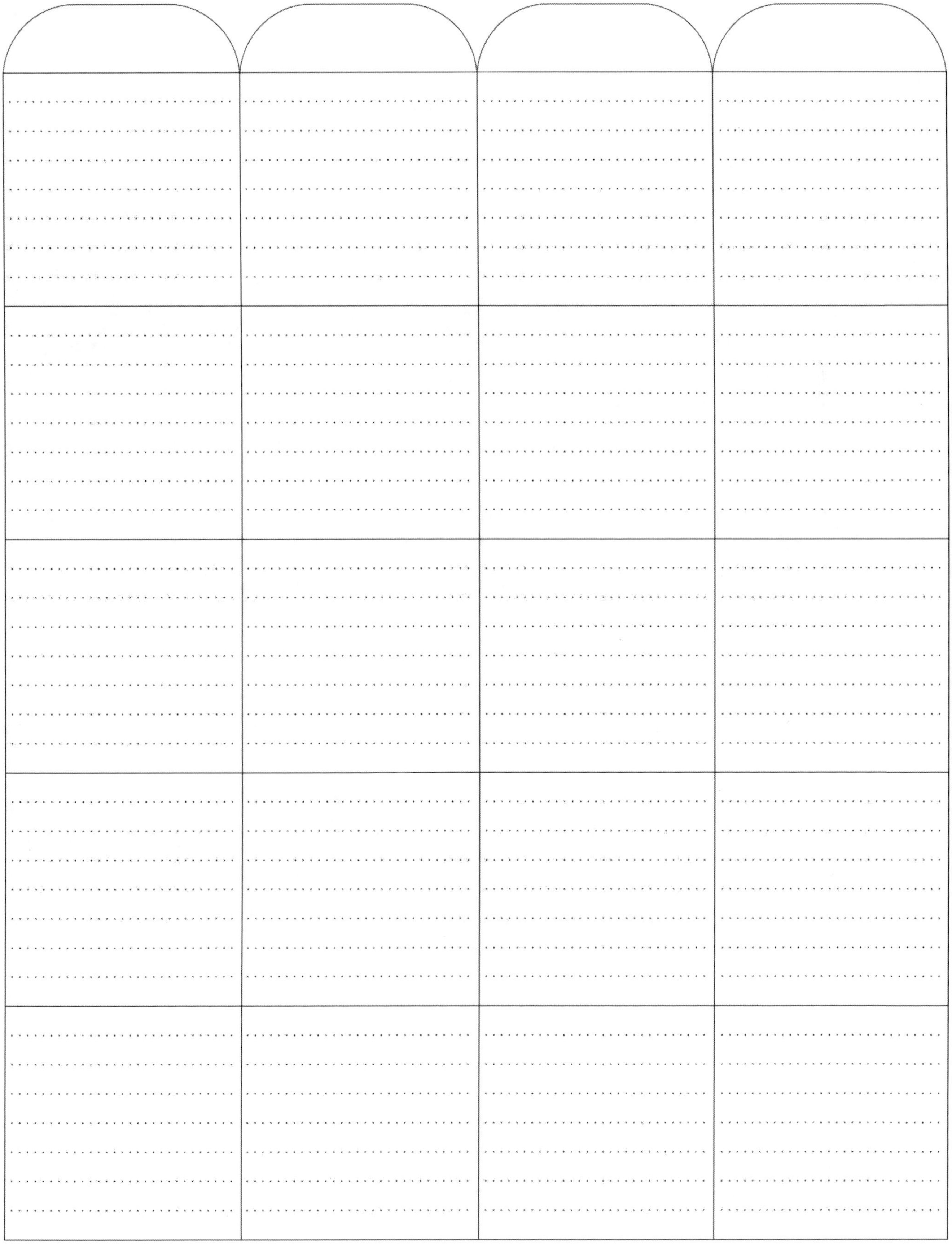

LESSON PLANNER

LESSON PLANNER

LESSON PLANNER

LESSON PLANNER

Self education is the only possible education, the rest is mere veneer laid on the surface of a child's nature

- Charlotte Mason

tracking

- Attendance
- Student Checklist
- Budget

attendance record

	1	2	3	4	5	6	7	8	9	10	11	12
1												
2												
3												
4												
5												
6												
7												
8												
9												
10												
11												
12												
13												
14												
15												
16												
17												
18												
19												
20												
21												
22												
23												
24												
25												
26												
27												
28												
29												
30												
31												
TOTAL												

student checklist

student checklist

student checklist

homeschool budget

EXPENSE	AMOUNT	DATE	NOTES
TOTAL			

homeschool budget

EXPENSE	AMOUNT	DATE	NOTES

TOTAL

Children learn from anything and everything they see. They learn wherever they are, not just in special learning places

- John Holt

review and reflect

- Year In Review
- Notes

year in review

OUR FAVORITE SUBJECTS THIS YEAR

BEST FIELD TRIP

BEST RESOURCE

BIGGEST ACCOMPLISHMENT

PLACES WE'VE SEEN

CLOSEST FRIENDS

GOALS FOR NEXT YEAR

photo collage

notes

notes

notes

notes

notes

notes